NANCY TUMINELLY

Cool | DAIRY-FREE RECIPES

DELICIOUS & FUN FOODS WITHOUT DAIRY

A Division of ABDO
ABDO
Publishing Company

visit us at www.abdopublishing.com

Published by ABDO Publishing Company, a division of ABDO, P.O. Box 398166, Minneapolis, Minnesota 55439. Copyright © 2013 by Abdo Consulting Group, Inc. International copyrights reserved in all countries. No part of this book may be reproduced in any form without written permission from the publisher. Checkerboard Library™ is a trademark and logo of ABDO Publishing Company.

Printed in the United States of America, North Mankato, Minnesota
102012
012013

 PRINTED ON RECYCLED PAPER

Design and Production: Mighty Media, Inc.
Series Editor: Liz Salzmann
Photo Credits: Aaron DeYoe, Shutterstock

The following manufacturers/names appearing in this book are trademarks:
Pyrex®, EZ-Foil®, Kitchen Aid®, Arm & Hammer®, Kraft® Calumet®, Ghirardelli®, Nestlé®, Skippy®, Enjoy Life®, Roundy's®, Coconut Dream®, Ancient Harvest®, Shedd's® Willow Run®, Crystal Sugar®, C&H®, Yehuda®, Osterizer®, Oster®, Proctor-Silex®

Library of Congress Cataloging-in-Publication Data

Tuminelly, Nancy, 1952-
 Cool dairy-free recipes : delicious & fun foods without dairy / Nancy Tuminelly.
     p. cm. -- (Cool recipes for your health)
 Audience: 8-12.
 Includes index.
 ISBN 978-1-61783-581-0
 1. Milk-free diet--Recipes. I. Title. II. Title: Dairy-free recipes.
 RM234.5.T86 2013
 641.5'63--dc23
                     2012024096

TO ADULT HELPERS

This is your chance to introduce newcomers to the fun of cooking! As children learn to cook, they develop new skills, gain confidence, and make some delicious food.

These recipes are designed to help children cook fun and healthy dishes. They may need more adult assistance for some recipes than others. Be there to offer help and guidance when needed, but encourage them to do as much as they can on their own. Also encourage them to be creative by using the variations listed or trying their own ideas. Building creativity into the cooking process encourages children to think like real chefs.

Before getting started, establish rules for using the kitchen, cooking tools, and ingredients. It is important for children to have adult supervision when using sharp tools, the oven, or the stove.

Most of all, be there to cheer on your new chefs. Put on your apron and stand by. Watch and learn. Taste their creations. Praise their efforts. Enjoy the culinary adventure!

CONTENTS

DAIRY-FREE

VEGAN is a term for people who don't eat *any* animal-**derived** products. This includes dairy, eggs, and meat. Many of the recipes in this book are vegan. Try them out on your friends!

LEARN MORE ABOUT COOKING DAIRY-FREE MEALS!

Following a dairy-free diet means that you don't eat anything made with milk from an animal. Some people don't eat dairy because they don't like the taste. Other people have a condition called *lactose intolerance.* That means eating dairy makes them feel sick.

There are a lot of foods for people who don't eat dairy. Try some of the dairy-free recipes in this book!

When shopping, look for fresh ingredients. Be sure to avoid things that might be made with dairy. Read the labels carefully.

Sometimes a recipe that includes dairy will list non-dairy **options** for those ingredients. Or, be creative and make up your own **variations**. Being a chef is all about using your imagination.

SAFETY FIRST!

Some recipes call for activities or ingredients that require caution. If you see these symbols, ask an adult for help!

Hot - This recipe requires handling hot objects. Always use oven mitts when holding hot pans.

Sharp - You need to use a sharp knife or cutting tool for this recipe. Ask an adult to help out.

Nuts - This recipe includes nuts. People who are allergic to nuts should not eat it.

THE BASICS

ASK PERMISSION

Before you cook, ask **permission** to use the kitchen, cooking tools, and ingredients. If you'd like to do something yourself, say so! If you would like help, ask for it!

BE NEAT AND CLEAN

- Start with clean hands, clean tools, and a clean work surface.
- Wear comfortable clothing.
- Tie back long hair and roll up your sleeves so they stay out of the food.

NO GERMS ALLOWED!

Raw eggs and raw meat have bacteria in them that can make you sick. After you handle raw eggs or meat, wash your hands, tools, and work surfaces with soap and water. Keep everything clean!

BE PREPARED

- Be organized. Knowing where everything is makes cooking easier!
- Read the directions all the way through before you start cooking.
- Set out all your ingredients before starting.

BE SMART, BE SAFE

- Never work alone in the kitchen.
- Ask an adult before using anything hot or sharp, such as a stove top, oven, knife, or **grater**.
- Turn pot handles toward the back of the stove to avoid accidentally knocking them over.

MEASURING

Many ingredients are measured by the cup, tablespoon, or teaspoon. Some ingredients are measured by weight in ounces or pounds. You can buy food by its weight too.

THE TOOL BOX

**9×9-INCH
BAKING PAN**

BAKING SHEET

BLENDER

COLANDER

CUTTING BOARD

ELECTRIC MIXER

FORK

FRYING PAN

MEASURING CUPS

MEASURING SPOONS

MIXING BOWLS

MIXING SPOON

The tools you will need for the recipes in this book are listed below. When a recipe says to use a tool you don't recognize, turn back to these pages to see what it looks like.

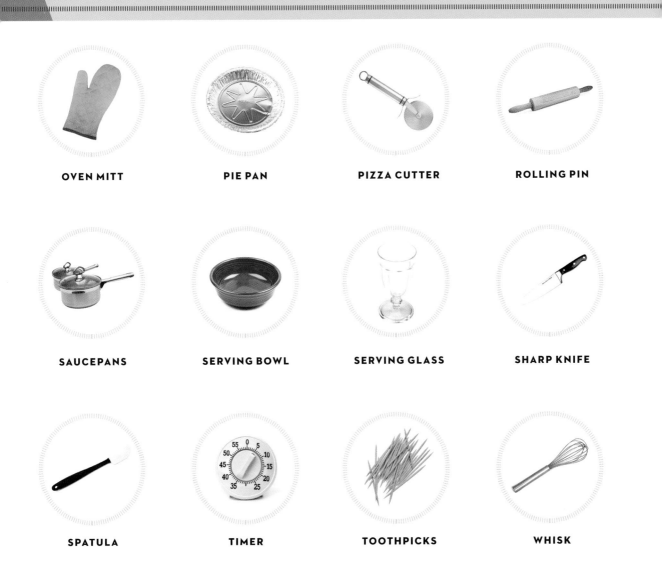

OVEN MITT

PIE PAN

PIZZA CUTTER

ROLLING PIN

SAUCEPANS

SERVING BOWL

SERVING GLASS

SHARP KNIFE

SPATULA

TIMER

TOOTHPICKS

WHISK

COOL INGREDIENTS

BAKING POWDER AND SODA

BANANAS

BROCCOLI

CASHEWS

CAYENNE PEPPER

CELERY

CINNAMON

CLEMENTINES

COCOA POWDER
(SWEETENED, UNSWEETENED)

CORNMEAL

CREAMY PEANUT BUTTER

DAIRY-FREE DARK CHOCOLATE CHIPS

EGGS

GARLIC

GROUND MUSTARD

HOT DOGS

Many of these recipes call for basic ingredients such as non-stick cooking spray, flour, salt, and black pepper. Here are other ingredients needed for the recipes in this book.

LEMON JUICE

MILK
(ALMOND, COCONUT, SOY)

NUTRITIONAL YEAST

OIL
(CANOLA, OLIVE, SESAME)

ONIONS
(RED, YELLOW)

PENNE PASTA

PEPPERS
(JALAPEÑO, RED BELL, THAI CHILI)

QUINOA

SOY MARGARINE

SOY SAUCE

STRAWBERRIES

SUGAR
(BROWN, POWDERED, WHITE)

TEHINA PASTE

TOFU

TURMERIC

VANILLA EXTRACT

COOKING TERMS

CHOP

Chop means to cut things into pieces using a knife.

CUBE

Cube means to cut something into medium-sized squares with a knife.

DICE

Dice means to cut something into small pieces with a knife.

DRAIN

Drain means to pour out all of the excess water.

FLUFF

Fluff means to loosen or separate pieces of something with a fork.

MIX

Mix means to stir ingredients together, usually with a large spoon.

PEEL

Peel means to remove the skin, often with a peeler.

SLICE

Slice means to cut food into pieces of the same thickness.

STIR-FRY

Stir-fry means to cook quickly in oil over high heat while stirring continuously.

TOSS

Toss means to turn ingredients over to coat them with seasonings.

PASTRY POCKETS

makes 6 pastries

INGREDIENTS

DOUGH

non-stick cooking spray

1½ cups all-purpose flour

½ teaspoon salt

½ cup soy margarine

¼ soy milk

FILLING

1¼ cups brown sugar

¾ cup powdered sugar

3 tablespoons all-purpose flour

1 tablespoon cinnamon

3½ tablespoons lemon juice

TOOLS

baking sheet

measuring cups & spoons

mixing bowls

spatula

oven mitts

rolling pin

pizza cutter

mixing spoon

timer

YOUR FRIENDS WILL LOVE THESE CINNAMON TREATS!

1. Preheat the oven to 450 degrees. Coat the baking sheet with cooking spray.

2. Put the flour, salt, and soy margarine in a large bowl. Mix with your hands until it is crumbly. Pour in the soy milk. Mix with a spatula until it is doughy.

3. Sprinkle flour on a clean surface. Place the dough on top. Flatten it with a rolling pin until it is $\frac{1}{8}$ inch (.3 cm) thick. Cut it into 12 rectangles with a pizza cutter.

4. Mix all of the filling ingredients together in a medium bowl.

5. Spread $1\frac{1}{2}$ tablespoons of filling on six of the dough rectangles. Leave a $\frac{1}{4}$-inch (.6 cm) border around the edges. Put the remaining six rectangles on top of the ones with filling. Pinch the edges together. Place the rectangles on the baking sheet.

6. Sprinkle them with brown sugar and bake for 10 minutes. Let them cool before eating them.

CHOCOLATE SHAKE

makes 2 servings

INGREDIENTS

2 bananas, sliced

2 cups soy milk

3 tablespoons sweetened cocoa powder

4 tablespoons cashews

2 strawberries

TOOLS

sharp knife

cutting board

measuring cups & spoons

blender

serving glass

1. Put the banana slices, soy milk, cocoa, and cashews in the blender. Press the lid on tightly.

2. Blend the ingredients on a low setting. Keep blending until the mixture is smooth and creamy.

3. Use a sharp knife to cut halfway through each strawberry, starting at the tip.

4. Put a strawberry on the rim of each glass for decoration. Pour the chocolate mixture into the glasses and serve.

TOFU SCRAMBLE

makes 4 servings

INGREDIENTS

2 tablespoons olive oil

3 cloves garlic, chopped

1½ cups yellow onion, chopped

3 tablespoons jalapeño pepper, chopped

1 red bell pepper, chopped

12-ounce package extra firm tofu, drained

⅓ cup nutritional yeast

2 tablespoons tehina paste

1 teaspoon turmeric

1 teaspoon salt

¼ teaspoon black pepper

¼ cup unsweetened soy milk

TOOLS

sharp knife

cutting board

measuring cups & spoons

blender

serving glass

1. Heat the olive oil in a large frying pan over medium-high heat. Add garlic and onion. Stir fry for about 4 minutes. Add the jalapeño and red pepper. Cook for another 4 minutes.

2. Put the tofu in a medium mixing bowl. **Crumble** it with your hands. Stir in the nutritional yeast and tehina paste. Add the turmeric, salt, and black pepper. Mix well.

3. Pour the tofu mixture into the frying pan with the vegetables. Stir all the ingredients together.

4. Add the soy milk. Cook until the liquid is gone. Remove the pan from the stove.

5. Divide into bowls and serve.

SUPER
BROCCOLI SALAD

makes 5 servings

INGREDIENTS

DRESSING

12-ounce package extra firm tofu, drained

2 tablespoons olive oil

2 tablespoons ground mustard

2 tablespoons lemon juice

1 tablespoon sugar

¼ teaspoon salt

SALAD

4½ cups broccoli

3 clementines

1 celery stalk, chopped

¼ cup red onion, chopped

1 cup cashews

TOOLS

measuring cups & spoons

blender

sharp knife

cutting board

large mixing bowl

forks

1. Put the tofu and olive oil in a blender. Blend on a low setting until smooth. Add the mustard, lemon juice, sugar and salt. Blend again for 45 seconds. This is the dressing.

2. Cut off the broccoli stem. Cut high enough to separate the broccoli **florets**. Cut each floret in half.

3. Peel the clementines. Separate the sections.

4. Put the broccoli florets, clementine sections, celery, onion, and cashews in a mixing bowl. Mix with two forks.

5. Pour the dressing over the vegetables and toss.

PEANUT NOODLES

makes 5 servings

INGREDIENTS

1 tablespoon sesame oil

2 large cloves garlic, finely chopped

2 or 3 Thai chili peppers, finely chopped

½ cup creamy peanut butter

3 tablespoons sugar

1½ tablespoons lemon juice

1 tablespoon soy sauce

¼ teaspoon cayenne pepper

¾ cup coconut milk

16 ounces penne pasta

TOOLS

measuring cups & spoons

small saucepan

sharp knife

cutting board

mixing spoons

timer

large saucepan

colander

large bowl

1. Heat the oil in a small saucepan over medium-high heat. Stir in garlic and Thai chili peppers. Cook for 4 minutes.

2. Add the peanut butter, sugar, and lemon juice. Stir until the sugar is fully **dissolved**.

3. Stir in the soy sauce, cayenne pepper, and coconut milk. Cook until warm. Remove from the heat and set aside.

4. Put 4 quarts of water in a large saucepan. Bring the water to a boil over high heat. Add the pasta and stir.

5. Wait for the water to begin boiling again. Then set the timer for the time shown on the package. Stir the pasta every few minutes while it is boiling.

6. Put the colander in the sink. Carefully pour the pasta into the colander to drain. Put the drained pasta in a large bowl. Pour the sauce over the pasta.

7. Stir until all the noodles are coated with sauce.

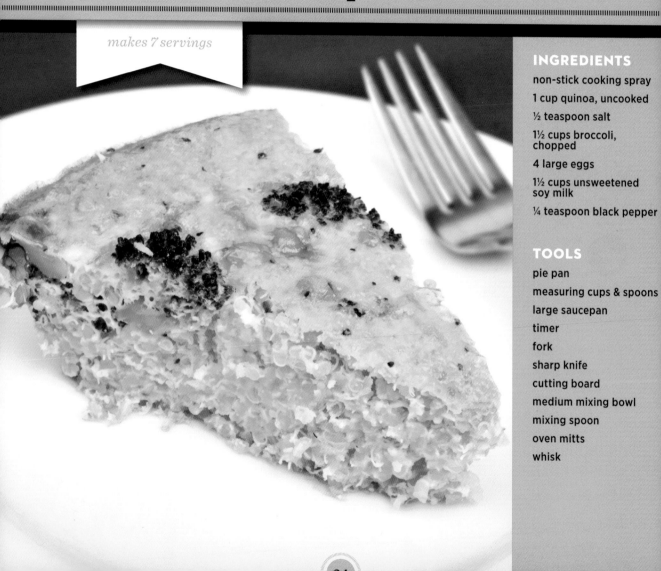

BAKED QUINOA

makes 7 servings

INGREDIENTS

non-stick cooking spray

1 cup quinoa, uncooked

½ teaspoon salt

1½ cups broccoli, chopped

4 large eggs

1½ cups unsweetened soy milk

¼ teaspoon black pepper

TOOLS

pie pan

measuring cups & spoons

large saucepan

timer

fork

sharp knife

cutting board

medium mixing bowl

mixing spoon

oven mitts

whisk

1. Preheat the oven to 350 degrees. Coat the pie pan with cooking spray.

2. Put 2 cups of water in a large saucepan. Add the quinoa and salt. Bring to a boil over medium-high heat. Then cover the pan and turn heat down to low.

3. Let the quinoa cook for 15 minutes. Most of the water should be absorbed.

4. Remove the saucepan from the heat. Fluff the quinoa with a fork. Add the broccoli. Stir gently. Cover the pan again and cook over the warm burner for about 5 minutes.

5. Crack the eggs into a mixing bowl. Whisk in the soy milk and pepper.

6. Pour the quinoa mixture into the pie pan. Pour the egg mixture over the top.

7. Bake for 45 minutes. Remove from oven. Cool for 10 minutes. Cut into wedges and serve.

MINI CORN DOGS

makes 48 pieces

INGREDIENTS

non-stick cooking spray

1 cup cornmeal

1 cup all-purpose flour

2 tablespoons brown sugar

1½ teaspoons baking powder

½ teaspoon baking soda

½ teaspoon salt

1 large egg

1¼ cups almond milk

2 teaspoons olive oil

16 hot dogs, cut in thirds

TOOLS

baking sheet

measuring cups & spoons

mixing bowls

mixing spoon

sharp knife

cutting board

toothpicks

timer

oven mitts

MAKE THIS BALLPARK FAVORITE AT HOME!

1. Preheat the oven to 400 degrees. Coat the baking sheet with cooking spray.

2. Put the cornmeal, flour, brown sugar, baking powder, baking soda, and salt in a large mixing bowl. Stir well.

3. Crack the egg into a small mixing bowl. Add the almond milk and olive oil. Stir until combined. Add the egg mixture to the cornmeal mixture. Stir well.

4. Stick a toothpick into one end of each hot dog piece. Dip each piece into the batter. Arrange them on the baking sheet.

5. Bake for 18 minutes. The dough should be puffy and golden brown. Remove them from the oven. Serve them while they're warm.

BROWNIE-WOWIES

makes 12 servings

INGREDIENTS

non-stick cooking spray

2 cups all-purpose flour

sugar

¾ cup unsweetened cocoa powder

1 teaspoon baking powder

1 teaspoon salt

1 cup mashed bananas

6 tablespoons unsweetened soy milk

6 tablespoons canola oil

1 teaspoon vanilla extract

1 cup dairy-free dark chocolate chips

powdered sugar

TOOLS

9×9-inch baking pan

measuring cups & spoons

mixing bowls

mixing spoon

electric mixer

timer

oven mitts

toothpick

1 Preheat the oven to 350 degrees. Coat the baking pan with cooking spray.

2 Put the flour, sugar, cocoa powder, baking powder, and salt in a medium mixing bowl. Stir them together.

3 Put the bananas, soy milk, canola oil, and vanilla in a small mixing bowl. Stir them together.

4 Add the banana mixture to the flour mixture. Mix with an electric mixer until thick. Add the chocolate chips. Stir with a mixing spoon.

5 Pour batter into the baking pan. Bake for 25 minutes. Remove pan from oven. Let it cool. Cut into 12 pieces. Sprinkle with powdered sugar.

HELPFUL TIP

Check to make sure the brownies are fully cooked by inserting a toothpick into the center. If the toothpick comes out clean, they are done!

more about DAIRY-FREE LIFE

If you liked these dishes, look for other dairy-free foods. If you want or need to avoid eating dairy, you have a lot of **options**!

Dairy ingredients are often used in cooking and baking. Keep your kitchen stocked with healthy, non-dairy **alternatives** for those ingredients. Some great dairy substitutes to try include soy milk, coconut milk, almond milk, butter substitute, and **sorbet**.

Now you're ready to start making your own dairy-free recipes. It takes creativity and planning. Check out different cookbooks. Look through the lists of ingredients. You'll be surprised how many dishes don't need dairy. Or you can come up with your own recipes or **variations**. The kitchen is calling!

Dairy products have important **nutrients**. If you're not eating dairy, be sure to get these nutrients from other sources. Eat foods such as broccoli, beans, and tofu for **calcium**. For extra **vitamin** D, spend more time out in the sun. But don't forget the sunscreen!

GLOSSARY

ALTERNATIVE - something you can choose instead.

CALCIUM - a natural element that is needed for good health, especially for healthy teeth and bones.

CRUMBLE - to break into small pieces.

DERIVE - to come from a certain source or basis.

DISSOLVE - to become part of a liquid.

FLORET - a piece of broccoli or cauliflower that does not include the stem.

GRATER - a tool with rough-edged holes used to shred something into small pieces.

INTOLERANCE - exceptional sensitivity to a drug or food.

LACTOSE - a sugar found in milk and other dairy products.

NUTRIENT - something that helps living things grow. Vitamins, minerals, and proteins are nutrients.

OPTION - something you can choose.

PERMISSION - when a person in charge says it's okay to do something.

SORBET - a fruit-flavored ice usually served as a dessert.

VARIATION - a change in form, position, or condition.

VITAMIN - a substance needed for good health, found naturally in plants and meats.

INDEX